YOUR KNOWLEDGE HAS V

- We will publish your bachelor's and
  master's thesis, essays and papers

- Your own eBook and book -
  sold worldwide in all relevant shops

- Earn money with each sale

Upload your text at www.GRIN.com
and publish for free

Bibliographic information published by the German National Library:

The German National Library lists this publication in the National Bibliography; detailed bibliographic data are available on the Internet at http://dnb.dnb.de .

Imprint:

Copyright © 2017 GRIN Verlag
Print and binding: Books on Demand GmbH, Norderstedt Germany
ISBN: 9783668888555

This book at GRIN:

https://www.grin.com/document/455229

Haitham Ismail

Ransomware life cycle and how to combat it

GRIN Verlag

GRIN - Your knowledge has value

Since its foundation in 1998, GRIN has specialized in publishing academic texts by students, college teachers and other academics as e-book and printed book. The website www.grin.com is an ideal platform for presenting term papers, final papers, scientific essays, dissertations and specialist books.

Visit us on the internet:

http://www.grin.com/

http://www.facebook.com/grincom

http://www.twitter.com/grin_com

DISTANCE LEARNING THROUGH ARDEN UNIVERSITY (RDI)

IN PARTIAL FULFILMENT OF THE REQUIREMENTS FOR THE DEGREE OF

MSc INFORMATION SYSTEMS (SYSTEMS SECURITY)

Concepts and Measures of Information Security Management

Q&A of Ransomware

SUBMITTED BY (HAITHAM ISMAIL)

Date for Submission: 20th July 2017 (14:00 BST)

Table of Contents

List of Figure

List of Tables

Part 1:

A. The Importance of Information Security

Information is an important asset for individuals, organisations, and governments. Stealing confidential information such as credit card numbers or Intellectual properties can cause financial loss or reputation damage. For example, Organisations invest in research creating intellectual property to secure their future earnings and pursue innovation (Casey, 2012). Because of that, Rao & Nayak (2014) state that intellectual property is valuable assets that need to be protected from theft or unauthorised access as it will cost mainly a severe financial loss. Chai, et al. (2016) state that individuals might be subjected to electronic bullying and harassments through internet social media like Facebook and Twitter. Most of the cases, protecting customer's information is protected by law which means that the theft of customer's sensitive information such as personal identifiable information (PII) and protected health information (PHI) will cause organisations to pay fines that consider also as a financial loss and reputation damage. In Healthcare industry, unauthorised modification on medical records can cause human life losses.

Hammondl (2013) states that effective information security addresses the security triad (Confidentiality, Integrity & Availability). Confidentiality grantees that sensitive information (e.g. PHI, PII, Credit card, etc.) accessed by those who have the authority to access them (Barham, 2010). On the other hand, Integrity is making sure that data is protected against unauthorised malicious or non-intention modifications (Hammondl, 2013). Finally, availability grantees that information is available for the right person when it's needed and access granted (Barham, 2010).

BBC (2017) reported in 12th of May an example that shows how important information security is to our life. Information security was violated by a massive cyber-attack hit NHS services across England and Scotland resulting hospital operation disruption and GP appointments that make staff uses pen and papers.

5

B. What is Ransomware, its history and how does it works?

A Ransomware attack is a malware outbreak whereby a type of malware is used to extort victims by taking their data as a hostage until their owners pay a certain amount of fee (Liska & Gallo, 2016). Mansfield-Devine (2016) states that it is a technological type of blackmailing by which malware on victim's mobiles or personal's computers encrypt or deny access to files and ask for money in exchange of the decryption key or allowing access, besides, payments are made by cyber-criminal currency Bitcoin that is hard to be tracked. It caused a monetary loss for enterprises by a total US$209 million in only the first three months last year (Trend Micro, 2016). Liska & Gallo (2016) state that the first Ransomware ever created known as AIDS that was written by Joseph Popp in 1984. In fact, its malicious code designed to replace the AUTOEXEC.BAT on the infected machines allowing only for 40 reboots before hiding all directories calming that it's encrypted. In 2005, the first modern ransomware that used symmetric encryption technique is released and it was known as GPCoder, its encryption was weak and easy to overcome (Richardson & North, 2017). In 2013, CryptoLocker was released by which it was encrypting files by the use of public and private keys and it was spreading when the victim click on a link appears to be from UPS (McDermott, 2015).

Liska & Gallo (2016) states that ransomware operation has several phases (See Figure 1, page 7) starting the deployment or installation phase. This installation is driven by convincing the victim to download malicious software by clicking a link in phishing emails or it uses unknown system vulnerability or in another name zero-day vulnerability for remote execution of the malware. Following that, it will start to establish connections (e.g. HTTP TOR), with its command servers as it collects information about the victim and its network, besides, identifying what to encrypt and where and exchange the encryption keys (Liska & Gallo, 2016). Afterwards, it encrypts the files and then payment is asked for decryption.

Deployment	Installation	Command-and-control	Destruction	Extortion
- Strategic web compromise - Drive-by downloads - Phishing (vishing or SMSishing) - Vulnerability exploitation	- Reconstruction - Process evasion - Memory access	- HTTP - Twitter - TOR - HTTPS - Email	- Encryption - Locking	- Bitcoin - Prepaid vouchers

Figure 1 - Anatomy of a Ransomware Attack (Liska & Gallo, 2016).

C. In-depth discussion of the vulnerability of the system which led to the wanacry ransomware attack

In April 2017, gigabytes of software exploits tools have been leaked from National Security Agency (NSA) by Shadow Broker, among these tools one tool called Eternal Blue was used to exploit a vulnerability found in Sever Message Block version 1 (SMB) which enable uploading code to a writable share and then load it into the memory and execute it (Goodin, 2017). The Eternal blue toolkit was used by Wannacry ransomware authors to exploit this vulnerability to replicate itself in the network (Sophos KB, 2017) like a worm. The Eternal Blue runs along with Eternal Rocks in a multistage process starting by a communication to command and control server through TOR browsing service to download and install additional exploit pack, following that, it starts to scan the local area network and the internet about opened port 445, then, it tries to repeat this process to other machines that have been found during the scan (Heller, 2017). In fact, Microsoft announced this vulnerability on March 14, 2017 by number MS17-010 and it released security critical update that will patch Microsoft different versions of windows against it by changing how SMBv1 handles specially crafted requests. (Microsoft , 2017). As per as this announcement, this vulnerability allows remote code execution and information disclosure and they have recommended disabling SMBv1 and relay on SMBv2 & SMBv3. Samani et al. (2017) state that by using MS17-010 vulnerability an attacker can gain access and escalate the privileges on a remote system in one step which mean that ransomware can control over the entire local area network who have not been updated by MS17-010 patch through infecting only one machine. Microsoft (2017) states that these vulnerabilities have been recorded in the Common Vulnerabilities and Exposures database by numbers CVE-2017-0148. All legacy operating systems (e.g. Windows XP, Windows 2003, etc.) are in lack of Windows security patches to be hardened from SMBv1 vulnerability as it is announced to be End of life (Microsoft, 2016). Furthermore, Linux is not a way of from this threats. Linux SMB vulnerability has been recorded in the Common Vulnerabilities and Exposures database by numbers from CVE-2017-7494 that have the same impact as CVE-2017-0148 of privileged remote code execution (CVE, 2017). Intrusion detection and preventions vendors were actively working to develop signatures for SMBv1 vulnerability to have better detection and prevention controls. For example, McAfee (2017a) state that they have developed urgent signature UDS detecting Eternal Blue remote code execution attack and it can prevent it.

Misconfigurations of the security controls are crucial. According to Malwarebytes Labs, Clark (2017) state that as a part of anti-sandbox technique the malware tries to connect to a website (www.iuqerfsodp9ifjaposdfjhgosurijfaewrwergwea.com), if it doesn't connect, it will not execute, so if the sandboxing technology is not configured to grant malware internet access, it will not detect the malware. In this case, sandboxing solution should grant malware execution process internet access or it will not detect it.

In conclusion, Wannacry ransomware attack makes use of leaked exploit toolkit to compromise platforms that are not patched against SMBv1 vulnerability (e.g. MS17-010), gain a privileged access and start to replicate itself with platforms that have similar circumstances. In addition, the Proper configuration for the security controls is crucial for detections and prevention against ransomware attacks.

D. The impacz of this type of attack on confidentiality, integrity and availability of data and resources being attacked

Stoneburner (2001) states in the National Institute of Standards and Technology special publication (NIST SP 800-33) clear definitions for the concepts of the security triad, he mentioned that Confidentiality of data and system information is to prevent disclosure or access of information from unauthorised individuals. However, integrity is the prevention of any unauthorised modifications. On the other hand, Availability is the assurance that systems and data work immediately and service has no denied to the authorised users. According to Mansfield-Devine (2016), Ransomware, in general, can completely bring down business operations (Wrights, 2016) which are considered a direct impact on the availability of service and information. For example in hospitals or healthcare providers, the ransomware on victim device (e.g. a server hold patients medical records) encrypt files on the hard drives and makes files not available or inaccessible and put human life in danger (Ayala, 2016). According to Malwarebytes (2017), wanncry malware will start privilege escalated scanning the network for vulnerable systems for SMBv1 with very law scanning profile to avoid scanning detection in a spreading attempt to convert the entire network hosts into zombies to C&C server before starting identifying files to encrypt and encryption of these files which means that the confidentiality of the network and its topology is violated and leaked. After the files have been identified, it encrypts a copy of these files in the destruction phase, while the original file is deleted or access denied which is a direct violation of availability (Clark, 2017). Furthermore, Liska & Gallo (2016) state that some ransomware makes files not accessible by making the applications that run unusable, for example, the ransomware display a full-screen window that covers the entire desktop that doesn't make it usable.

In addition, ransomware will gain full privileged access to choose and encrypt (Samani, et al., 2017) whatever is valuable to the victim that is considered an unauthorised access which led to the disclosure of the information. In fact, the ransomware after deployment and installation phase will try to establish a connection with a command and control server (C&C). Liska & Gallo (2016) states that it will wait for instructions (e.g. download exploit tools, execute commands, etc.) and sometimes report to its server with a huge amount of information the local systems (e.g. IP addresses range, domain name, file types, files locations, etc.). Indeed, Ionita & Patriciu (2016) state that once the victim is connected to C&C servers that can do either the rest of the wanncry ransomware anatomy or any other thing even a DDOS attack as it becomes a zombie. In 2013, a dangerous exploit tool, PassFreely, has been leaked by shadow broker (same who leaked eternal blue) and used to bypass Oracle database authentication in memory permitting unauthenticated sessions to Oracle instance with version 11.2.0.1 on windows server 2008 R2 (Rashid, 2017). So, If we consider that both tools have been leaked by shadow brokers the same mysterious online group that leaked Eternal blue that are the main components in the Wanncry ransomware and the fact that Wanncry ransomware receives instructions from C&C server, PassFreely could be downloaded and executed. Rashid (2017) states that if the compromised machine is a Windows server platforms that carry out Oracle database which is unpatched against PassFreely exploit, wanncry authors might have access to Oracle database that is a direct violation of integrity and confidentiality.

In conclusion, ransomware has a severe impact on the security triad CIA (e.g. Confidentiality, Integrity and Available). it affects availability by the destruction of the original files either by deleting or denying access or corrupting applications that run the files. In addition, it violet confidentiality and integrity by having privileged escalated access through eternal blue tools that exploit the SMBv1 vulnerability and have the right to access and modify all files on the hard drive and memory. Finally, victim machine might receive instructions to download another tool that can make exploit to other application that is running on the infected system (e.g. PassFreely).

Part 2:

Discussion of basic guidelines and security safeguard measures that can be applied to this scenario to mitigate the chances of future attack

In general, most of the security threats can be overcome by a defense in depth architecture by which a layers of defensive controls (See Figure 2, Page 12) is used to deter attacker from gaining unauthorized access (e.g. NAT, DMZ-firewall, IDS/IPS, patched host, AV, etc.), besides, it protect against advanced organized attack (e.g. Adaptive Persistent Threats) that has the ability to use zero-day vulnerability (Cleghorn, 2013).

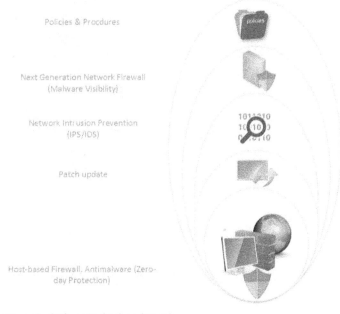

Policies & Procdures

Next Generation Network Firewall
(Malware Visibility)

Network Intrusion Prevention
(IPS/IDS)

Patch update

Host-based Firewall, Antimalware (Zero-
day Protection)

Figure 2 - Defense In-depth architecture

Liska & Gallo (2016) state that ransomware attack in phases (See Figure 1, Page 7), we can defend against ransomware by preventing activities related to each phase. Initially, ransomware is deployed by vulnerability exploitation, phishing emails and driven by downloads. If we applied defense in depth architecture, full patched hardened host will prevent initial infection that exploits vulnerable SMBv1 systems (Samani, et al., 2017) or harden the host by disabling unnecessary services (e.g. disable SMBv1 if not needed),

11

deploying patches (e.g. Windows patches[1], applications patches), implement host-based firewall (e.g. host based firewall policies allowing only trusted sources from contacting to the host), and proper configuration of the required service must take priority when planning to secure primse (Stallings & Brown, 2012 cited in Cleghorn, 2013). The second attack vector is phishing email, and to prevent them Kanthety (2010) state that the increase of users security awareness to understand what is phishing attacks and its risk helps in phishing mitigations, besides, it can be mitigated by using properly configured email gateway that can block spoofed emails and internet proxy that block access to suspicious sites and block malicious downloads. McAfee (2017b) states that blocking malicious downloads can be controlled by integrating internet proxy with sandboxing technology by which internet proxy or web gateway inspect the traffic and threat blocking through a series of malware detection methodology that used for zero-day malware detection and can be provided by sandboxing (e.g. McAfee Advanced Threat Defense) technology provided in real-time, besides, it can also be integrated with other network security platforms (See Figure 3, Page 14) to enhance security like Intrusion prevention systems, email gateway, web gateway, endpoint antivirus, etc. Next phase of ransomware is installation, Symantec (2015) states that unknown malware or zero days malware that doesn't have virus definition available can be blocked by file reputation lookup by which unknown file has no reputation withing the organisation so it will not be executed. Another technique is based on file behaviour. For example, McAfee (2016b) introduced Dynamic application containment feature by which any suspicious file will be blocked based on the behaviour that malware usually uses.

---

[1] MS17-010 fix the vulnerability that used by wannacry to be infect other machine

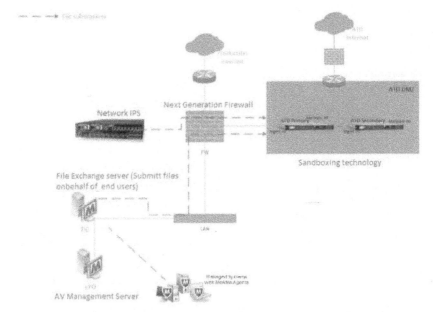

Figure 3 - Fully Integrated anti-malware solution.

Third ransomware infection phase is C&C, Victim machine tries to initiate a callback connection to receive instruction and start ransomware activity through Tor service. By using network IPS and next-generation firewall we can block high-risk application such as Tor traffic and any peer to peer traffic (PaloAlto, 2013) to block the communication between infected machines and C&C servers. If the ransomware starts encryption, Mcafee (2017c) states that it will try to create an encrypted file with an extension of .wcry extension and this can be blocked by blocking the creation of files with unknown extensions which can be done by the endpoint security solution like McAfee (McAfee, 2016a) or PaloAlto traps.

The last stage of the ransomware is to block access to legitimate file and ask for ransom we can overcome this stage by having a regular backup of client data (Alge, 2016).

In Summary, each of the ransomware phases has specific actions that can be stopped by certain security controls (See Table 1, Page 14). From deployment till ransom pathing through installation, C&C, and destruction phases, if any activity in any stage stopped, ransomware life cycle will be stopped and it waits it for this activity to be completed to move to the next activity. However, implementation of all of this controls should be guided by implementation of good information security policy to help business objective of keeping information safe and available.

Ransomware Phase	Activity	Security control
Deployments	Vulnerability exploitation	Defence in depth strategy/Periodically patc deployments/disable unnecessary services/ho based firewall/
	Phishing Emails	Security Awareness campaigns/Email Gateway block spoofed email
	Download	Sandboxing integrated with different securi appliances (Internet Proxy, Network IP Endpoint security, etc)
Installations	Download additional components Installation of additional components	Implement File Reputation and Behavior analys antivirus
Command & Controls (C&C)	Call back activity	Block Tor & P2P activity by IPS & Ne generation firewall
Encryption	Create files with unknown extensions (e.g. winry)	Using EndPoint protection solution unknown specific file extension can be blocked fro creation
Ransom	Deny access to files	Restore the previous backup

Table 1- Defending against ransomware

Reference list

Alge, W., 2016. Best practice for defending against ransomware. [Online] Available at: http://go.galegroup.com.ezproxy.liberty.edu/ps/i.do?p=GRGM&u=vic_liberty&id=G ALE|A469209702&v=2.1&it=r&sid=summon&authCount=1 [Accessed 11 June 2017].

Ayala, L., 2016. Cybersecurity for Hospitals and Healthcare Facilities.[Online],Virginia, USA: Apress.

Barham, C., 2010. Confidentiality and security of information. Anaesthesia & Intensive Care Medicine, [Online], 11(12), pp. 502-504.

BBC, 2017. NHS cyber-attack: GPs and hospitals hit by ransomware. [Online] Available at: http://www.bbc.com/news/health-39899646 [Accessed 27 May 2017].

Casey, B. 2012. The Impact of the Intellectual Property Theft on the Economy. [Online] Available at: https://www.jec.senate.gov/public/_cache/files/aa0183d4-8ad9-488f-9e38-7150a3bb62be/intellectual-property-theft-and-the-economy.pdf [Accessed 27 May 2017]

Chai, S. et al., 2016. Role of perceived importance of information security: an exploratory study of middle school children's information security behavior. Informing Science & Information Technology, [Online], 3(1), p. 127.

Clark, Z., 2017. The worm that spreads WanaCrypt0r. [Online] Available at: https://blog.malwarebytes.com/threat-analysis/2017/05/the-worm-that-spreads-wanacrypt0r/ [Accessed 2 June 2017].

Cleghorn, L., 2013. Network Defense Methodology: A Comparison of Defense in Depth and Defense in Breadth. Journal of Information Security, [Online], 4 (1), pp. 144-149

CVE, 2017. CVE-2017-7494. [Online] Available at: http://cve.mitre.org/cgi-bin/cvename.cgi?name=CVE-2017-7494 [Accessed 31 June 2017].

Goodin, D., 2017. NSA-leaking Shadow Brokers just dumped its most damaging release yet. [Online] Available at: https://arstechnica.com/security/2017/04/nsa-leaking-shadow-brokers-just-dumped-its-most-damaging-release-yet/ [Accessed 31 May 2017].

Hammondl, M. W., 2013. How Do Your IT Controls Measure Up Against The Information Security Triad?. IT Security, [Online], p. 13.

Heller, M., 2017. Seven NSA cyberweapons used in EternalRocks exploit. [Online] Available at: http://searchsecurity.techtarget.com/news/450419517/Seven-NSA-cyberweapons-used-in-EternalRocks exploit?utm_medium=EM&asrc=EM_NLN_77904342&utm_campaign=20170531_S amba vulnerability could lead to WannaCry-like attacks for Linux,

Unix&utm_source=NLN&track=N
[Accessed 1 June 2017].

Ionita, M.-G. & Patriciu, V.-V., 2016. Defending Against Attacks from the Dark Web. International Journal of Computer Science and Information Security, [Online], 14(7), pp. 226-237.

Kanthety, S. S., 2010. Prevention of Phishing Attacks using Link-Guard Algorithm. International Journal of Computer Science Issues, [Online], 7(2), pp. 31-36.

Liska, A. & Gallo, T., 2016. Ransomware.[Online],California, US: O'Reilly Media, Inc.Mansfield-Devine, S., 2016. Ransomware: taking businesses hostage. Network Security, [Online], 1(1), pp. 8-17.

McAfee, 2016a. Fie/folder blocking. [Online] Available at: https://kc.mcafee.com/corporate/index?page=content&id=KB81095 [Accessed 11 June 2017].

McAfee, 2016b. Unmask Evasive Threats. [Online] Available at: https://www.mcafee.com/us/resources/white-papers/wp-real-protect-dynamic-application-containment.pdf [Accessed 10 June 2017].

McAfee, 2017a. McAfee SNS Notice: Network Security Platform Emergency UDS Release Bulletin. [Online] Available at: https://kc.mcafee.com/corporate/index?page=content&id=SNS690&actp=null&viewl ocale=en_US&showDraft=false&platinum_status=false&locale=en_US [Accessed 1 June 2017].

McAfee, 2017b. Advanced Threat Detection analysis for gateway. [Online] Available at: https://www.mcafee.com/us/resources/solution-briefs/sb-atd-web-gateway.pdf[Accessed 10 June 2017].

McAfee, 2017c. McAfee_Labs_WannaCry_May_24. [Online] Available at: https://kc.mcafee.com/resources/sites/MCAFEE/content/live/PRODUCT_DOCUME NTATION/27000/PD27077/en_US/McAfee_Labs_WannaCry_May_24.pdf [Accessed 11 June 2017].

McDermott, I. E., 2015. Ransomware: a tales from CrytpoLocker. Online searcher, [Online], 1(1), pp. 35-37.

Microsoft, 2016. Windows XP support has ended. [Online] Available at: https://support.microsoft.com/en-us/help/14223/windows-xp-end-of-support [Accessed 1 June 2017].

Microsoft , 2017. Microsoft Security Bulletin MS17-010 - Critical. [Online] Available at: https://technet.microsoft.com/en-us/library/security/ms17-010.aspx [Accessed 31 May 2017].

PaloAlto, 2013. How to Create an Application Filter to Block High-Risk Applications. [Online] Available at: https://live.paloaltonetworks.com/t5/Configuration-Articles/How-to-Create-an-Application-Filter-to-Block-High-Risk/ta-p/62794 [Accessed 10 June 2017].

Rao, U. H. & Nayak, U., 2014. The InfoSec Handbook: An Introduction to Information Security. [Online]:Apress.

Rashid, F. Y., 2017. WannaCry ransomware slipped in through slow patching. [Online] Available   at http://go.galegroup.com.ezproxy.liberty.edu/ps/i.do?p=ITOF&u=vic_liberty&id=GA LE|A491763164&v=2.1&it=r&sid=summon&authCount=1 [Accessed 5 June 2017].

Richardson, R. & North, M., 2017. Ransomware: Evolution, Mitigation and Prevention. International Management Review, [Online], 13(1), pp. 10-21.

Samani, R., Beek, C. & McFarland, C., 2017. An Analysis of the WannaCry Ransomware Outbreak. [Online] Available at: https://securingtomorrow.mcafee.com/executive-perspectives/analysis-wannacry-ransomware-outbreak/ [Accessed 31 May 2017].

Schwartz, M. J., 2016. PassFreely Attack Bypasses Oracle Database Authentication. [Online] Available at: http://www.bankinfosecurity.com/passfreely-attack-bypasses-oracle-database-authentication-a-9868 [Accessed 5 June 2017].

Stoneburner, G., 2001. Underlying Technical Models for Information Technology Security (NIST SP 800-33), [Online], Gaithersburg: U.S. Department of Commerce, Available at: http://csrc.nist.gov/publications/nistpubs/800-33/sp800-33.pdf [Accesse15d 3 June 2017]

Sophos KB, 2017. Wana Decrypt0r 2.0 Ransomware. [Online] Available at: https://community.sophos.com/kb/en-us/126733 [Accessed 31 May 2017].

Symantec, 2015. Protection from Advanced Threats with Symantec™ Insight and SONAR. [Online] Available at: https://www.symantec.com/content/dam/symantec/docs/other-resources/protection-from-advanced-threats-with-symantec-insight-and-sonar.pdf [Accessed 10 June 2017].

Trend Micro, 2016. The reign of ransomware. [Online] Available at: 'The reign of ransomware'. Trend Micro. Accessed Sep 2016. www. trendmicro.com/cloud-content/us/ pdfs/security-intelligence/reports/ rpt-the-reign-of-ransomware.pdf. [Accessed 29 May 2017].